Lima Beans

Cookbook

Introduction

Lima beans have been grown in Peru for the past 9,000 years. It is named after Peru's capital, Lima. The plant's proper name, "lunatus," means "half-moon" and refers to the shape of the bean. Potatoes, quinoa, and lima beans were staple products during the Incan empire in the Andes region.

Beans are packed with protein, fiber, and other nutrients, making them a superfood. Lima beans are an especially good source of iron. One cup of lima beans contains roughly one quarter of your daily recommended iron.

Lima beans are sometimes called butter beans, especially in the Southern United States. Lima beans can be fried, sauteed or baked. They can be used in casseroles, put in soups or added to a bean mixture known as succotash.

Succotash is a vegetable dish consisting primarily of sweet corn with lima beans or other shell beans. Other ingredients may be added, such as onions, potatoes, turnips, tomatoes, bell peppers, corned beef, salt pork, or okra.

This book has many lima bean recipes for every day of the year. Enjoy!

Sautéed Lima Beans and Onions

Ingredients:

Cooking spray
1/2 medium onion, finely chopped
1 1/2 cups chicken broth
1 (16 oz.) package frozen baby lima beans

Directions:

1. Heat a large saucepan over medium heat, and spray with cooking spray.
2. Sauté onions until soft and translucent.
3. Pour in chicken broth, and bring to a boil.
4. Add lima beans, and enough water just to cover.
5. Bring to a boil, then reduce heat to low, cover, and simmer for 30 minutes, until beans are tender.

Southern Lima Beans and Ham

Ingredients:

1 pound dried baby lima beans
2 quarts water
2 onions, coarsely chopped
1 meaty ham bone
1 cup leftover ham meat from bone, chopped
3 cups water, or as needed to cover
1 tsp. Cajun seasoning
1/4 tsp. freshly ground black pepper
1/4 tsp. garlic salt, or to taste
1 pinch cayenne pepper

Directions:

1. Soak lima beans in 2 quarts of water in a large bowl for 8 hours or overnight. The next day, drain the lima beans and place into a slow cooker with onions, ham bone, and ham.
2. Pour in 3 cups of water or as needed to cover.
3. Place lid on the cooker, set to High, and cook for 3 hours.
4. Stir in Cajun seasoning, black pepper, garlic salt, and cayenne pepper; set cooker to Low and cook until the beans and meat are very tender, about 4 more hours.

Gigantes (Greek Lima Beans)

Ingredients:

1 (16 oz.) package dried lima beans
2 (16 oz.) cans chopped tomatoes with juice
1 cup olive oil
3 cloves garlic, chopped
1 tsp. chopped fresh dill
sea salt to taste
1 cup water, or as needed (Optional)

Directions:

1. Place lima beans into a large saucepan and add enough water to cover by 2 inches. Soak for 8 hours or overnight.
2. When ready to cook, preheat the oven to 375 degrees F (190 degrees C).
3. Place the saucepan with beans and water over medium heat and bring to a boil.
4. Reduce the heat to medium-low and simmer for 20 minutes.
5. Drain beans; pour into a 9x13-inch baking dish.
6. Add tomatoes, olive oil, garlic, dill, and salt; stir to combine.
7. Bake in the preheated oven, stirring occasionally and adding water if the mixture appears dry, until beans are tender, 1 1/2 to 2 hours.

Lima Bean Soup

Ingredients:

1 pound dry lima beans
4 cups water
5 carrots, chopped
1 leek, bulb only, chopped
2 tbsps. minced shallots
2 stalks celery, chopped
4 cubes vegetable bouillon
8 cups water
2 tbsps. olive oil

Directions:

1. Bring 4 cups of water to a boil.
2. Add dry lima beans, and boil for 2 to 3 minutes.
3. Remove from heat, and allow the beans to sit, covered, for 1 to 2 hours to soften.
4. Drain and rinse until water runs clear, discarding bean water.
5. In a soup pot, sauté vegetables in olive oil until onions and celery are translucent.
6. Add lima beans, and sauté for another 2 to 3 minutes.
7. In the meantime, bring 4 cups of water to a boil.
8. Add the vegetable bouillon to the boiling water, and stir until dissolved.
9. Add broth to the sautéed vegetables and beans.
10. Add remaining water, and allow soup to simmer over a low flame for 1 to 1 1/2 hours.
11. Serve steaming hot.

Lima Bean Soup with Ham

Ingredients:

1 ham bone with some meat
8 cups water, plus more as needed
1 (16 oz.) package dried lima beans
1 tbsp. olive oil
4 stalks celery, diced
1 onion, diced
1/2 pound diced cooked ham
4 carrots, peeled and sliced
1 tsp. salt
1 tsp. ground black pepper
1 tsp. dried parsley

Directions:

1. Combine ham bone and 8 cups water in a large saucepan. Simmer over medium-low heat until remaining meat falls off the bone, about 2 hours.
2. Remove and discard bone.
3. Use a slotted spoon to transfer meat to a bowl.
4. Meanwhile, place lima beans in a large pot; pour in enough cold water to cover.
5. Bring to a boil; remove pot from heat, cover, and let stand for 1 hour.
6. Drain and rinse beans.
7. Heat oil in a skillet over medium heat.
8. Add celery and onion; cook and stir until onion is translucent, 5 to 7 minutes.
9. Add cooked ham bone meat, lima beans, and diced ham.
10. Reduce heat and simmer, adding additional water as needed, until soup is thickened to desired consistency, about 90 minutes.
11. Stir carrots, salt, pepper, and parsley into the soup.
12. Let simmer until carrots are soft, about 30 minutes more.

Pork and Lima Beans

Ingredients:

2 tbsps. garlic powder
2 tbsps. onion powder
1 tbsp. cayenne pepper
1 tbsp. rubbed sage
1 tbsp. ground nutmeg
1 tsp. seasoned salt
salt and pepper to taste
3 pounds pork neck bones
3 tbsps. olive oil
1 cup diced onion
1 cup chopped red bell pepper
1 (16 oz.) package dried lima beans
10 cups water, divided

Directions:

1. Combine the garlic powder, onion powder, cayenne pepper, sage, nutmeg, seasoned salt, salt, and pepper in a small bowl. Rub 3/4 of this mixture into the pork neck bones; set the neck bones and remaining seasoning aside.
2. Heat the olive oil in a large skillet over medium heat.
3. Stir in the onion and bell pepper; cook and stir until the onion has softened and turned translucent, about 5 minutes.
4. Add the neck bones; reduce heat to low, and cover.
5. Cook, stirring occasionally, for 1 hour, adding water as needed to keep the meat and vegetables from scorching.
6. Meanwhile, place the lima beans into a large pot and pour in 8 cups of water; bring to a boil over high heat.
7. Once boiling, turn off the heat, cover, and let stand 1 hour.
8. After the beans have stood for 1 hour, drain and rinse. Return the beans to the pot, and pour in 2 cups of water.
9. Bring to a boil over high heat, then stir in the pork and vegetables, and the remaining spice mixture.

10. Reduce heat, cover, and simmer until the lima beans are tender, and the pork is falling off the bones, about 30 minutes.

Creole Chicken Stew with Baby Lima Beans

Ingredients:

4 slices reduced-sodium bacon
1 3/4 pounds boneless, skinless chicken thighs
salt and ground black pepper to taste
1 medium onion, chopped
1 medium green bell pepper, chopped
2 stalks celery, chopped
3 cloves garlic, minced
1 pound frozen lima beans
1 (14.5 oz.) can crushed fire-roasted tomatoes
1 cup chicken broth
2 tsps. Creole seasoning, or to taste

Directions:

1. Brown bacon in a 4-quart chef's pan or sauté pan over medium heat, 4 to 6 minutes.
2. Drain on paper towels.
3. Season chicken thighs with salt and pepper and add to the bacon drippings in the pan. Brown over medium heat, about 4 minutes per side.
4. Remove from the pan and set aside.
5. Add onion, bell pepper, celery, and garlic to the same pan and cook in the drippings over medium heat, stirring occasionally, until tender, 4 to 5 minutes.
6. Meanwhile, cut browned chicken thighs into bite-sized pieces and chop the browned bacon.
7. Add to the vegetables once tender.
8. Stir in frozen baby lima beans, crushed tomatoes, and chicken broth.
9. Season with Creole seasoning and adjust salt and pepper, if necessary.
10. Press lima beans down into the cooking broth so they cook evenly.

11. Bring to a boil, reduce heat to medium-low, and cook uncovered, stirring every 5 to 10 minutes, until chicken is cooked through, 20 to 25 minutes. An instant-read thermometer inserted into the center of the chicken should read at least 165 degrees F (74 degrees C).

Salmon Corn Chowder with Lima Beans

Ingredients:

1/4 pound sliced bacon, cut crosswise into thin strips
1 onion, chopped
1 1/4 pounds boiling potatoes, peeled and cut into 1/2-inch cubes
3 cups canned low-sodium chicken broth or homemade stock
1 3/4 tsps. salt
2 ⅔ cups fresh or frozen corn kernels
1 pound skinless salmon fillets, cut into 1-inch pieces
1 cup frozen baby lima beans, thawed
1/8 tsp. fresh-ground black pepper
3/4 cup half-and-half
2 tbsps. chopped chives or scallion tops

Directions:

1. In a large pot, cook the bacon until crisp.
2. Remove with a slotted spoon and drain on paper towels.
3. Pour off all but 1 tbsp. of fat from the pot.
4. Add the onion and cook over moderately low heat, stirring occasionally, until translucent, about 5 minutes.
5. Add the potatoes, broth, bacon, and 1/2 tsp. of the salt to the pot and simmer, covered, for 10 minutes.
6. Put the corn kernels in a food processor and pulse six to eight times to chop.
7. Add the corn to the pot and cook, covered, until the potatoes and corn are just done, about 5 minutes longer.
8. Add the salmon, lima beans, the remaining 1 1/4 tsps. salt, and the pepper.
9. Bring just back to a simmer; the fish should be just cooked through.
10. Stir in the half-and-half and serve the chowder topped with the chives.

Mediterranean Lima Beans

Ingredients:

2 tbsps. extra-virgin olive oil
2 cups chopped fresh or frozen onions
4 cloves garlic, minced
1 tsp. dried oregano
1 tsp. ground cinnamon
1/2 tsp. crushed red pepper, or to taste
2 (14 oz.) cans diced tomatoes
2 (10 oz.) packages frozen baby lima beans

Directions:

1. Heat oil in a large nonstick skillet over medium-high heat.
2. Add onions and cook, stirring occasionally, until soft, 3 to 5 minutes.
3. Add garlic and cook 1 minute more.
4. Stir in oregano, cinnamon, crushed red pepper, tomatoes and lima beans.
5. Cook, stirring occasionally, until the beans are fully cooked and the mixture is heated through, 10 to 15 minutes.
6. Serve hot.

Greek Lima Beans

Ingredients:

1 (10 oz.) package frozen baby lima beans
1 cup water
3 tbsps. extra-virgin olive oil
2 tbsps. Chopped fresh flat-leaf parsley
1 tbsp. minced garlic
1/2 tsp. salt

Directions:

1. Cook lima beans, water, 2 tbsps. oil, 1 tbsp. parsley, garlic, and salt in a 2-quart heavy saucepan, tightly covered, over moderate heat, stirring occasionally, until beans are tender, 17 to 20 minutes.
2. Season with salt and pepper and transfer to a bowl.
3. Serve sprinkled with remaining tbsp. parsley and drizzled with remaining tbsp. oil.

Chorizo Lima Beans

Ingredients:

3 tbsps. extra-virgin olive oil, divided
2 medium carrots, minced
1 large red onion, peeled and minced
1 1/2 tbsps. minced fresh thyme
1/4 tsp. crushed red pepper
3 oz. reduced-fat Spanish-style chorizo, finely diced (see Tip)
3 (10 oz.) packages frozen baby lima beans
1 cup dry white wine
1/2 cup reduced-sodium chicken broth
3 cloves garlic, minced
1 tbsp. sherry vinegar
1/2 tsp. kosher salt

Directions:

1. Heat 1 tbsp. oil in a large saucepan over medium heat.
2. Add carrots, onion, thyme and crushed red pepper and cook, stirring, until beginning to brown, 6 to 8 minutes.
3. Stir in chorizo and cook, stirring occasionally, until heated through, about 5 minutes more.
4. Add lima beans, wine, broth and garlic and cook for 5 minutes, scraping up any browned bits.
5. Cover and cook over medium-low heat for 20 minutes.
6. Remove from the heat and stir in the remaining 2 tbsps. oil, vinegar and salt.
7. Let stand for at least 10 minutes before serving.

Southern Butter Beans

Ingredients:

1 (16 oz.) package dried lima beans
5 slices bacon, chopped
1 cup heavy whipping cream
1/2 cup butter
Salt and ground black pepper to taste

Directions:

1. Place lima beans in a large pot.
2. Cover with water and soak overnight.
3. Drain and return lima beans to the pot; cover beans with fresh water.
4. Heat a large skillet over medium-high heat; cook and stir bacon in the hot skillet until crisp, about 5 minutes.
5. Use a slotted spoon to remove bacon to a paper towel-lined plate to drain. Reserve about 2 tsps. bacon drippings.
6. Add bacon and reserved bacon drippings to lima beans in the pot; bring to a boil.
7. Reduce heat to medium-low and simmer until beans are just tender, 40 to 60 minutes.
8. Stir heavy cream and butter into bean mixture and cook until thickened, about 15 minutes more.
9. Season with salt and pepper.

Lima Bean Dip

Ingredients:

1 (15 oz.) can lima beans, drained and rinsed
⅔ cup nonfat sour cream
1 clove garlic, crushed
2 tbsps. sun-dried tomato paste
5 drops Few drops Tabasco sauce
1 tsp. fresh lemon juice
1/4 oz. fresh basil leaves
1 pinch Salt and fresh-ground pepper
8 oz. baby carrots
8 oz. baby corn, blanched 1 minute and drained, then halved lengthwise
1 small red bell pepper, seeded and cut into strips
1 small yellow bell pepper, seeded and cut into strips
4 stalks celery stalks, cut into 3-inch strips
4 pita breads
8 sesame-seed breadsticks

Directions:

1. Place the lima beans, sour cream, garlic, tomato paste, Tabasco sauce, and lemon juice in a food processor or blender. Reserve one basil leaf for garnishing, and add the rest to the food processor or blender. Blend to a smooth puree, scraping down the sides of the container once or twice.
2. Season with salt and pepper to taste. Spoon into a bowl and garnish with the reserved basil leaf.
3. Cover and chill while preparing the crudities.
4. Heat the broiler. Prepare all the vegetables and arrange them on a large serving platter.
5. Warm the pitas under the broiler 1 to 2 minutes, then cut into wedges.
6. Add to the vegetable platter with the sesame breadsticks.
7. Serve with the dip.

Veal Loin with Fennel-Lima Bean Puree

Ingredients:

1 (16 oz.) package dried lima beans
2 garlic cloves, minced
2 medium fennel bulbs-halved, cored and finely chopped, plus
2 tbsps. minced fennel fronds
1/2 small onion, minced
1 tsp. finely grated lemon zest
4 pounds boneless veal loin, tied at 2-inch intervals with kitchen string
1 pinch Salt and freshly ground pepper
1/2 cup Dijon mustard blended with
1/2 cup creme fraiche
10 sage leaves
1 1/2 tsps. fennel seeds, lightly toasted and finely ground

Directions:

1. In a large saucepan, cover the limas with 4 inches of water and bring to a boil. Simmer over low heat for 1 hour, then add water to cover by 2 inches.
2. Add the garlic, chopped fennel, onion and lemon zest. Boil over moderately high heat for 15 minutes, stirring often.
3. Reduce the heat to low and simmer, stirring occasionally, until the lima beans and fennel become a thick and creamy puree, about 2 hours.
4. Meanwhile, preheat the oven to 450 degrees F.
5. Season the veal roast with salt and pepper and set it, fat side down, on a rack set in a medium roasting pan.
6. Spread half of the mustard cream over the veal and top with half of the sage leaves.
7. Put the roast in the oven, reduce the temperature to 300 degrees F and roast for 45 minutes.
8. Carefully turn the veal fat side up; spread with the remaining mustard cream and top with the remaining sage leaves. Roast the veal for 1 hour longer, or until an instant-read

thermometer inserted in the thickest part of the meat registers 145 degrees F.

9. Transfer the veal roast to a carving board to rest for 10 minutes.
10. Stir the ground fennel seeds into the fennel-lima puree.
11. Season with salt and pepper. Discard the kitchen string and slice the meat thickly.
12. Transfer the veal to plates and spoon the fennel-lima puree alongside.
13. Garnish with the fennel fronds.

Steak and Lima Bean Rice

Ingredients:

2 tbsps. vegetable oil, divided
1 (10 oz.) package frozen baby lima beans, thawed
2 (15 oz.) cans tomato sauce
1 cup boiling water
⅓ cup white sugar
2 pounds beef top round steaks, 3/4 inch thick
1/4 cup all-purpose flour
salt and pepper to taste
2 cups uncooked long grain rice
4 cups water

Directions:

1. Heat 1 tbsp. of oil in a large saucepan over medium heat.
2. Add the lima beans, and cook until wrinkled, about 10 minutes.
3. Pour tomato sauce over the beans and stir in 2 cups of water and sugar.
4. Cover and simmer over low heat for 45 minutes.
5. Heat the remaining tbsp. of oil in a large skillet over medium-high heat. Brown steaks on each side, then pour in just enough water to cover.
6. Place a lid on the pan and simmer for 35 to 40 minutes over medium-low heat. Spoon some of the liquid into a cup or small bowl and mix with flour until smooth. Return to the pan and simmer until gravy has thickened.
7. Season with salt and pepper to taste.
8. Combine the rice and 4 cups water in a saucepan.
9. Bring to a boil, then reduce heat to low.
10. Cover and cook for 20 minutes, or until rice is tender.
11. To serve, spoon rice onto plates.
12. Top with steak and gravy then top with lima bean sauce.

Bar-B-Q Bean Medley

Ingredients:

1 (15 oz.) can kidney beans, drained (Optional)
1 (15 oz.) can pinto beans, drained
1 (15 oz.) can lima beans, drained
1 (16 oz.) can great Northern beans, drained
1 (12 oz.) bottle chili sauce
2 tbsps. brown sugar
1 tbsp. Dijon mustard
1 tbsp. Worcestershire sauce
2 tbsps. molasses
3 slices bacon, cut in half

Directions:

1. Preheat oven to 325 degrees F (165 degrees C).
2. In a medium baking dish, mix kidney beans, pinto beans, lima beans, great northern beans, chili sauce, brown sugar, Dijon mustard, Worcestershire sauce and molasses.
3. Top with bacon.
4. Bake 1 hour in the preheated oven, until thick and bubbly.

Chicken, Corn and Lima Bean Stew

Ingredients:

2 tbsps. vegetable oil
2 medium onions, diced
1 green bell pepper, ribs and seeds removed, diced
1 tbsp. chopped fresh thyme
1 pinch Coarse salt and ground pepper
2 tbsps. tomato paste
1 1/2 pounds boneless, skinless chicken thighs
6 plum tomatoes, diced
1/4 cup Worcestershire sauce
1 (10 oz.) package frozen corn kernels, thawed
1 (10 oz.) package frozen lima beans, thawed

Directions:

1. Heat oil in a Dutch oven (or other 5-quart pot) over medium-high heat.
2. Add onions, bell pepper, thyme, 11/2 tsps. salt, and1/4teaspoon pepper.
3. Cook, stirring occasionally, until onions begin to brown, 4 to 5minutes.
4. Stir in tomato paste; add chicken, tomatoes, Worcestershire sauce, and 11/2 cups water.
5. Bring to a boil; reduce to a simmer.
6. Cover, and cook until chicken is opaque throughout, about 15 minutes.
7. Remove chicken from pot; stir in corn and lima beans, and simmer until heated through, about 5 minutes.
8. Meanwhile, shred chicken meat with your fingers or a fork. Return chicken to pot, and stir to combine.

Calico Beans Casserole

Ingredients:

1 pound lean ground beef
1/2 cup bacon, chopped
1 (15 oz.) can pork and beans
1 (15 oz.) can kidney beans, drained
1 (15 oz.) can butter beans
1 (15 oz.) can lima beans, drained
1 cup packed brown sugar
1 cup chopped onion
1/2 cup chopped celery
1/2 cup ketchup
3 tbsps. white wine vinegar
1 tsp. mustard powder

Directions:

1. Preheat the oven to 350 degrees F (175 degrees C).
2. Cook ground beef and bacon in a large, deep skillet over medium-high heat until evenly brown.
3. Drain and transfer meat to a 4-quart casserole dish.
4. Add pork and beans, kidney beans, butter beans, lima beans, brown sugar, onion, celery, ketchup, vinegar, and dry mustard to the casserole dish; mix well.
5. Bake, covered, in the preheated oven until bubbly and heated through, about 1 hour.

Pan-Fried Butter Beans

Ingredients:

3 tbsps. olive oil
1 (15 oz.) can butter beans - drained, rinsed, and patted dry
2 cloves garlic, peeled and bruised, or more to taste
2 sprigs fresh rosemary
1 pinch red pepper flakes, or more to taste
salt and ground black pepper to taste
1 tbsp. white wine vinegar

Directions:

1. Heat olive oil in a non-stick skillet over medium-low heat.
2. Cook and stir beans into hot oil until slightly golden and crispy, about 10 minutes.
3. Stir garlic, rosemary, red pepper flakes, salt, and black pepper into beans; continue cooking until crispy, about 5 minutes. Drizzle vinegar over beans and toss.

Brunswick Stew

Ingredients:

4 oz. diced salt pork
2 pounds chicken parts
8 cups water
3 potatoes, cubed
3 onions, chopped
1 (28 oz.) can whole peeled tomatoes, chopped
2 cups canned whole kernel corn
1 (10 oz.) package frozen lima beans
1 tbsp. Worcestershire sauce
1/2 tsp. salt
1/4 tsp. ground black pepper

Directions:

1. In a large pot over high heat, combine the salt pork, chicken and water and bring to a boil.
2. Reduce heat to low, cover and simmer for 45 minutes, or until chicken is tender.
3. Remove chicken and allow to cool until easy to handle.
4. Remove meat and discard the skin and bones. Chop meat into bite size pieces and return to the soup.
5. Add the potatoes, onions, tomatoes, corn, lima beans, Worcestershire sauce, salt and ground black pepper.
6. Stir well and simmer, uncovered, for 1 hour.

Creamy Succotash

Ingredients:

4 oz. thick sliced bacon, cut into 1/2-inch pieces
1 medium onion, cut into medium dice
1 (10 oz.) package frozen baby lima beans
Salt and freshly ground black pepper, to taste
1 (10 oz.) package frozen sweet corn
1/2 cup heavy cream
1 1/2 tsps. minced fresh thyme leaves
2 tsps. snipped fresh chives

Directions:

1. Fry bacon over medium-high heat in a Dutch oven until crisp, 7 to 8 minutes.
2. Using a slotted spoon, transfer bacon to a paper towel-lined plate.
3. Pour off all but 2 Tbs. of the bacon drippings.
4. Add onions; sauté until tender, about 5 minutes.
5. Add lima beans, 1/2 cup water, salt and pepper, and bring to a boil.
6. Reduce heat and continue to simmer, covered, until partially cooked, about 5 minutes.
7. Add corn, cream, and thyme; return to a simmer, and warm until vegetables are fully cooked and cream doesn't pool, about 5 minutes longer. (Can be refrigerated at this point up to 2 days ahead.)
8. When ready to serve, stir bacon and chives into warm succotash. This recipe doubles easily.

Mexican Succotash

Ingredients:

1 pound ground turkey
1 medium red bell pepper, chopped
1 medium green bell pepper, chopped
1 medium onion, chopped
1 1/2 cups water
1 (8 oz.) jar taco sauce
1 (1 oz.) package taco seasoning mix
1 (15 oz.) can corn, drained
1 (15 oz.) can baby lima beans, drained

Directions:

1. Heat a large skillet over medium-high heat.
2. Cook and stir turkey in the hot skillet until browned and crumbly, 5 to 7 minutes.
3. Add peppers and onion; cook and stir until soft, about 5 minutes.
4. Pour in water, taco sauce, and taco seasoning.
5. Stir together.
6. Reduce heat to a simmer and cook about 10 minutes.
7. Add corn and lima beans to pan and stir.
8. Let simmer until lima beans are tender and heated through, about 5 minutes more.

Picnic Baked Bean Casserole

Ingredients:

2 (15 oz.) cans pork and beans
1 (16 oz.) can kidney beans, rinsed and drained
1 (15 oz.) can lima beans, rinsed and drained
1 onion, chopped
1/2 cup packed brown sugar
1/2 cup ketchup
1/2 tsp. dry mustard
4 strips cooked bacon, crumbled

Directions:

1. Preheat oven to 350 degrees F (175 degrees C).
2. Grease a 2 1/2-quart baking dish.
3. Combine pork and beans, kidney beans, lima beans, onion, brown sugar, ketchup, and dry mustard together in a bowl; transfer to the prepared baking dish.
4. Sprinkle bacon over bean mixture.
5. Cover dish with aluminum foil.
6. Bake in the preheated oven for 30 minutes.
7. Remove aluminum foil and continue baking until bubbling, about 30 minutes more.

Beer and Bacon Butter Beans

Ingredients:

1 pound dried large lima beans (butter beans)
1 pound bacon
4 cups water, or more as needed
1 (12 fluid oz.) can or bottle beer
1/2 tsp. ground cumin (Optional)
1/2 jalapeno pepper, seeded and minced
1 clove garlic, minced

Directions:

1. Place beans into a large container and cover with several inches of cool water; let stand 8 hours to overnight.
2. Place bacon in the open pressure cooker and cook over medium-high heat, turning occasionally, until evenly browned, about 10 minutes.
3. Drain bacon slices on paper towels and remove pressure cooker from heat, reserving the bacon grease in the pressure cooker to cool, about 10 minutes.
4. Stir 4 cups water into cooled bacon grease; add beer and cumin.
5. Drain and rinse the soaked beans and add to the water mixture in the pressure cooker.
6. Place the lid on the pressure cooker and secure tightly.
7. Cook beans according to manufacturers' instructions for 15 psi over medium-high heat, about 30 minutes; release the pressure.
8. Stir jalapeno pepper and garlic into beans. Crumple bacon over beans.
9. Close pressure cooker again and bring to 15 psi over medium heat and immediately turn off heat.
10. Remove pressure cooker from heat and allow pressure naturally decrease to 0 psi.

Okra Lima Bean Soup

Ingredients:

4 cups chopped tomatoes
2 cups lima beans
2 cups chopped okra
2 cups chopped red potatoes
1 cup corn
1 cup green beans
1/2 cup chopped carrots
1 (6 oz.) can tomato paste
4 cups chicken stock
1 pound ground beef
1/2 tbsp. garlic powder
1/2 tbsp. celery salt
1/2 tbsp. onion powder
1 small onion, chopped
2 cloves garlic, crushed, or more to taste
3 tbsps. butter

Directions:

1. Combine tomatoes, lima beans, okra, potatoes, corn, green beans, carrots, and tomato paste in a large soup pot.
2. Pour chicken stock over mixture and bring to a boil over medium heat.
3. Reduce heat and simmer until vegetables begin to soften, about 15 minutes.
4. Season ground beef with garlic powder, celery salt, and onion powder.
5. Set aside.
6. Heat butter in a skillet over medium-high heat.
7. Add onion and garlic when butter stops bubbling; cook and stir for 1 minute.
8. Spread ground beef evenly in the pan.
9. Cook until it has a nice brown sear, stirring minimally to end up with mostly medium-sized chunks, 5 to 7 minutes.
10. Drain skillet and add beef, onions, and garlic to the soup pot.

11. Bring soup mixture to a boil; reduce heat to simmer, cover, and cook until vegetables and beef have cooked down, 1 to 2 hours.

Roasted Beet, Crab and Vegetable Soup

Ingredients:

4 beets, scrubbed, stems trimmed to 1 inch
2 tbsps. olive oil
salt and freshly ground pepper, to taste
2 tbsps. fresh lemon juice, or to taste
2 tbsps. olive oil
1 onion, chopped
2 tbsps. garlic, minced
1/2 cup chopped celery
1 (8 oz.) can sliced mushrooms
2 (13.75 oz.) cans chicken broth
1/2 (9 oz.) package frozen baby lima beans
1/2 (14 oz.) package frozen mixed vegetables
2 (14.4 oz.) cans diced tomatoes
1/2 (15 oz.) can peas
1/2 pound imitation crab meat, flaked
2 tsps. dried thyme
1 dash Louisiana-style hot sauce, or to taste
Salt and freshly ground pepper, to taste
2 tsps. fresh lemon juice, or to taste

Directions:

1. Preheat oven to 400 degrees F (200 degrees C).
2. Place beets into a 9x13 inch baking dish. Drizzle with 2 tbsps. olive oil and lemon juice.
3. Season with salt and pepper to taste.
4. Cook beets in preheated oven, turning occasionally, until fork tender, about 45 minutes.
5. Remove from oven, cool, peel, and cut into 1/2 inch pieces.
6. Heat 2 tbsps. olive oil in a large pot over medium heat.
7. Stir in the onion, garlic, celery, and mushrooms; cook and stir until the onion becomes transparent, about 5 minutes.
8. Pour in the chicken broth, and heat 5 minutes.

9. Add the lima beans and mixed vegetables; bring soup to a boil over high heat.
10. Reduce heat to medium-low, and stir in the tomatoes, peas, beets, and crab meat.
11. Season with thyme, hot sauce, salt, and pepper, to taste. Simmer 10 minutes more, and turn off the heat. Just before serving, stir in 2 tsps. lemon juice.

Meatless Chili

Ingredients:

1 (28 oz.) can crushed tomatoes
1 (8 oz.) container firm tofu, drained and cut into 1/2-inch cubes
3 cups water
1 1/2 cups chopped bell peppers
1 1/4 cups drained canned corn kernels
1 1/4 cups chopped carrots
1/2 cup Peppers, hot chili, green, canned, pods, excluding seeds, solids and liquids
1 tbsp. onion powder
1 1/2 tsps. garlic powder
1 1/2 tbsps. chili powder
1 1/2 tbsps. ground cumin
1 (15 oz.) can kidney beans, rinsed and drained
1 (15 oz.) can lima beans, drained
1 tbsp. original or unsweetened Almond Breeze Almond milk

Directions:

1. Combine tomatoes, tofu, water, bell peppers, corn, carrots, chile peppers, onion powder, garlic powder, chili powder, and cumin in a large pot over high heat; bring to a boil.
2. Reduce heat and simmer until vegetables are tender, 30 to 45 minutes.
3. Add kidney and lima beans; continue simmering until heated through, 10 to 15 minutes.
4. If chili sauce is too watery, stir in vegetable protein until desired thickness is reached.

Ground Beef and Vegetable Soup

Ingredients:

2 tbsps. olive oil
2 large yellow onions, diced
6 stalks celery, cut into 1/2-inch pieces
4 carrots, sliced 1/8-inch thick
3 cloves garlic, chopped
2 1/2 pounds lean ground beef
46 oz. low-sodium vegetable juice
46 oz. reduced-sodium beef broth
1 (28 oz.) can diced tomatoes
1 tbsp. Italian seasoning
2 cubes beef bouillon
1 tsp. ground thyme
1/4 tsp. cayenne pepper
Salt and pepper to taste
1 (15.25 oz.) can yellow corn, drained
1 (15.25 oz.) can red kidney beans, drained and rinsed
1 (15 oz.) can cannellini beans, drained and rinsed
1 (15 oz.) can great Northern beans, drained and rinsed
1 (14.5 oz.) can cut green beans, drained
8 oz. frozen peas
8 oz. frozen lima beans
8 oz. frozen sliced okra

Directions:

1. Heat olive oil in a large pot over medium heat.
2. Cook and stir onion, celery, and carrots until tender, 6 to 8 minutes.
3. Stir garlic into onion mixture; cook, stirring, until fragrant, about 1 minute.
4. Remove pot from heat.
5. Heat a large skillet over medium-high heat.
6. Cook and stir ground beef in batches in the hot skillet until browned and crumbly, 5 to 10 minutes.
7. Transfer browned beef to onion mixture in the large pot using a slotted spoon.

8. Heat onion-beef mixture over medium heat.
9. Stir vegetable juice, beef broth, tomatoes, Italian seasoning, beef bouillon, thyme, cayenne pepper, salt, and black pepper into beef mixture.
10. Bring to a boil, reduce heat to low, cover, and simmer to blend the flavors, at least 1 hour.
11. Stir corn, kidney beans, cannellini beans, great Northern beans, green beans, peas, lima beans, and okra into beef mixture; bring to a boil, reduce heat to low, and simmer until heated through, about 10 minutes.

Colorful Four Bean Salad

Ingredients:

1 cup white sugar
1 cup white vinegar
1 tbsp. vegetable oil
6 stalks celery, chopped
1 green bell pepper, seeded and chopped
1 medium red onion, chopped
1 (4 oz.) jar pimento peppers, drained and chopped
1 (14 oz.) can cut green beans
1 (14.5 oz.) can yellow wax beans
1 (15 oz.) can lima beans
1 (15 oz.) can dark red kidney beans

Directions:

1. In a large bowl, whisk together the white sugar, vinegar, and vegetable oil.
2. Stir in the celery, green pepper, red onion and pimentos.
3. Pour the green beans, wax beans, lima beans and kidney beans into a colander, and rinse under cold water.
4. Let drain for a few minutes, then stir into the bowl with the rest of the salad.
5. Store in a large jar in the refrigerator, and shake or turn occasionally for 1 day to marinate. If you do not have a sealed container, simply stir the salad every few hours. This keeps for about a week, but will be gone sooner.

Three Bean Salad

Ingredients:

1 cup frozen cut green beans
1 cup frozen lima beans
1 cup drained and rinsed canned red beans
1/2 cup frozen red bell pepper strips
1/2 cup chopped onion
2 tbsps. canola oil
1/4 cup apple cider vinegar
2 tsps. white sugar
1/2 tsp. garlic powder
Salt and ground black pepper to taste

Directions:

1. Combine green beans, lima beans, red beans, red bell pepper, and onion in a large bowl with a tight-fitting lid.
2. Mix together canola oil, apple cider vinegar, sugar, garlic powder, salt, and black pepper in a small bowl.
3. Pour mixture over bean mixture. Seal lid and shake bowl until evenly coated.
4. Refrigerate for 24 hours or until all ingredients are completely thawed.
5. Shake well before serving.

Hearty Fish Chowder

Ingredients:

2 medium potatoes, chopped
1 cup chopped onion
2 cloves garlic, minced
1 (10.75 oz.) can condensed cream of celery soup
1 (10 oz.) package frozen whole kernel corn
1 (10 oz.) package frozen baby lima beans
1 1/2 cups chicken broth
⅓ cup dry white wine or chicken broth
1 tsp. lemon-pepper seasoning
1 pound fresh or frozen cod or other whitefish fillets
1 (14.5 oz.) can stewed tomatoes, undrained
⅓ cup nonfat dry milk powder
1 tinfoil liner

Directions:

1. Line a 5- to 6-quart slow cooker with a tinfoil liner. Open slow cooker liner and place it inside a slow cooker bowl. Fit liner snugly against the bottom and sides of bowl; pull top of liner over rim of bowl.
2. Combine potatoes, onion, garlic, cream of celery soup, corn, lima beans, broth, white wine and lemon-pepper seasoning.
3. Cover and cook on low-heat setting for 6 to 7 hours or on high-heat setting for 3 to 3 1/2 hours.
4. Meanwhile, thaw fish if frozen. Rinse fish; pat dry with paper towels.
5. Place fish on the mixture in the cooker. If using low-heat setting, turn to high-heat setting.
6. Cover and cook for 1 hour more.
7. Add undrained tomatoes and nonfat dry milk powder to cooker, stirring gently to break up the fish.
8. Carefully remove lid to allow steam to escape.
9. Serve directly from slow cooker liner using a wooden or plastic utensil. Do not lift or transport liner with food inside.
10. Cool slow cooker completely; remove liner and toss.

Creole Catfish Stew

Ingredients:

2 tbsps. cooking oil
1 onion, chopped
2 ribs celery, cut into 1/2-inch pieces
1 green bell pepper, cut into 1/2-inch strips
1 tsp. dried thyme
1/2 tsp. dried oregano
1/2 tsp. dry mustard
1/2 tsp. Tabasco sauce
1/2 tsp. fresh-ground black pepper
1 tsp. salt
1/2 cup dry white wine
1 3/4 cups canned crushed tomatoes in thick puree
3 cups canned low-sodium chicken broth or homemade stock
2 cups frozen baby lima beans
2 cups fresh or frozen corn kernels
2 (10 oz.) fillets catfish fillets, cut into 1 1/2-inch pieces
2 tbsps. chopped fresh parsley

Directions:

1. In a large pot, heat the oil over moderate heat.
2. Add the onion, celery, and bell pepper and cook, stirring occasionally, until the onion is translucent, about 5 minutes.
3. Stir in the thyme, oregano, mustard, Tabasco sauce, pepper, and 1/2 tsp. of the salt.
4. Add the wine and cook until almost evaporated, about 4 minutes.
5. Add the tomatoes and broth to the pot and bring to a boil.
6. Reduce the heat and simmer, partially covered, for 10 minutes.
7. Add the lima beans and simmer for 3 minutes.
8. Stir in the corn and simmer 4 minutes more.
9. Add the catfish and the remaining 1/2 tsp. salt, bring back to a simmer, and cook until just done, about 2 minutes.
10. Serve topped with the parsley.

Porotos Granados (Chilean Bean Stew)

Ingredients:

1 tbsp. olive oil
1 yellow onion, chopped
2 cups cubed butternut squash
1 (15 oz.) can great Northern beans, rinsed and drained
1 cup frozen lima beans
3 cups chicken stock
2 cups frozen corn
2 tbsps. chopped fresh basil
1 banana pepper, chopped

Directions:

1. Heat the olive oil in a stock pot over medium heat; add the onion and cover.
2. Cook the onions until soft and translucent, about 5 minutes.
3. Stir the squash, great Northern beans, and lima beans into the pot; pour the chicken stock over the mixture.
4. Cover and cook until the squash is tender and beginning to break apart, 30 to 45 minutes.
5. Stir the corn and basil into the stew; cook until the stew reaches the consistency of pancake batter, about 10 minutes more.
6. Sprinkle the chopped banana pepper over individual portions to serve.

Green Bean and Butter Bean Salad

Ingredients:

2 pounds fresh green beans, ends snapped
1 pinch Salt
20 oz. butter beans, or small fresh or frozen lima beans
1/4 cup tarragon vinegar or white-wine vinegar
3 tbsps. Dijon mustard
1 pinch Freshly ground black pepper
1 shallot, minced
3/4 cup extra-virgin olive oil
2 tbsps. chopped fresh tarragon, plus more for garnish
2 tbsps. chopped fresh flat-leaf parsley, plus more for garnish

Directions:

1. Prepare an ice-water bath.
2. Cook green beans in boiling salted water, just until bright green and tender, about 5 minutes. Reserving the cooking liquid, remove beans with a large slotted spoon; transfer to ice-water bath to stop the cooking.
3. Transfer beans to a colander.
4. Cook butter beans in the boiling cooking liquid, just until tender, 5 minutes if frozen.
5. Strain; place under cold, running water to stop cooking.
6. Set aside.
7. Make vinaigrette: In a medium bowl, combine vinegar, mustard, salt and pepper to taste, and minced shallot.
8. Whisk in olive oil until vinaigrette is creamy.
9. Whisk in tarragon and parsley.
10. In a large bowl, toss green beans until well coated with about three-quarters of the vinaigrette.
11. In a large bowl or on a platter, arrange the green beans in an even layer.
12. Sprinkle the reserved butter beans over the top. Drizzle the remaining vinaigrette over the beans.
13. Garnish with tarragon and parsley.
14. Serve at room temperature.

Tuna and Pasta Salad

Ingredients:

3 cups rotelle pasta
3 hard-cooked eggs, chopped
1 (12 oz.) can tuna, drained and flaked
3/4 cup shredded Cheddar cheese
3/4 cup chopped celery
1/4 cup finely chopped onion
1/2 cup roasted red peppers, drained and chopped
1 (8 oz.) can lima beans, drained
3/4 cup mayonnaise
1/2 lemon, juiced
1/2 tsp. paprika
Salt to taste

Directions:

1. Bring a large pot of lightly salted water to a boil.
2. Add pasta and cook for 8 to 10 minutes or until al dente; drain and cool.
3. In a large bowl, combine pasta, eggs, tuna Cheddar cheese, celery, onion, roasted red pepper, and lima beans.
4. Whisk together mayonnaise, lemon juice, and paprika.
5. Season with salt.
6. Pour dressing over pasta mixture, and mix together.

Maryland Crab Soup

Ingredients:

2 (14.5 oz.) cans stewed tomatoes
3 cups water
2 cups beef broth
1 cup fresh lima beans
1 cup frozen corn kernels
1 cup sliced carrots
2 tbsps. chopped onion
2 tbsps. Old Bay Seasoning
1 gallon water
10 blue crab claws, steamed (Optional)
1 pound blue crab crabmeat

Directions:

1. Place stewed tomatoes, 3 cups water, beef broth, lima beans, corn, sliced carrots, chopped onion, and Old Bay seasoning in a 4-quart pot.
2. Bring to a simmer over medium heat; cover and cook for 5 minutes.
3. Bring 1 gallon water to a boil in a large pot.
4. Add crab claws and boil for 6 minutes; drain.
5. Stir crabmeat and boiled crab claws into tomato and vegetable mixture.
6. Cover and simmer for 10 to 15 minutes.
7. Serve hot.

Slow Cooker Beef Round Stew

Ingredients:

1 cup all-purpose flour
salt, to taste
ground black pepper, to taste
2 pounds beef round steak, cubed
3 tbsps. vegetable oil, or as needed
8 oz. fresh mushrooms, chopped
1 large onion, chopped
1 cup chopped carrot
4 cups beef broth, divided
2 (.87 oz.) packages dry brown gravy mix
1 large potato, cubed
1/4 cup frozen peas
1/4 cup frozen corn
1/4 cup frozen lima beans
1/4 cup frozen cut green beans
1 (10.75 oz.) can condensed cream of mushroom soup

Directions:

1. Place the flour in a shallow bowl, and mix with salt and black pepper.
2. Sprinkle beef with more salt and black pepper. Press the beef cubes into the seasoned flour, and tap off the excess flour.
3. Heat the vegetable oil in a large skillet over medium heat, and cook the beef cubes until browned on all sides, working in batches.
4. Place the browned beef into a slow cooker.
5. Place the mushrooms, onion, and carrot in the skillet with the last batch of meat; place in the slow cooker.
6. Pour about 1 cup of beef broth into the skillet, and stir to dissolve any brown bits left in the bottom of the skillet.
7. Pour into the slow cooker.
8. In a saucepan over medium heat, whisk the remaining beef broth with the dry gravy mix until smooth.

9. Bring the gravy to a boil, reduce heat to medium low, and simmer until thickened, about 2 minutes.
10. Stir the gravy into the stew.
11. Mix in the potato, frozen peas, corn, lima beans, and green beans. If you prefer a thicker gravy, mix in the cream of mushroom soup.
12. Place the lid on the cooker, set to low heat, and cook until the beef is very tender, about 4 hours. You can cook the stew up to 8 hours if necessary.

Lima Beans, Cabbage and Smoked Sausage

Ingredients:

1 (16 oz.) package dried lima beans, soaked overnight
2 smoked ham hocks
8 cups water
5 cups shredded cabbage
1/2 cup butter
1 1/2 tsps. salt
3/4 tsp. ground black pepper
3/4 tsp. garlic powder
1 (28 oz.) can diced tomatoes
1 pound smoked sausage, sliced (Optional)

Directions:

1. In a large pot, combine the lima beans, ham hocks, water, cabbage and butter.
2. Season with salt, pepper and garlic powder.
3. Bring to a boil, then reduce heat to low and set a lid on top but leave a crack for steam. Simmer for 1 1/2 hours.
4. Remove the lid, add the tomatoes and sausage; simmer with the lid on until beans are completely tender, 15 to 20 minutes.

Stewed Oxtails

Ingredients:

4 pounds beef oxtails, cut into pieces
2 onions, cut into large chunks
3 green onions, cut into large pieces
1 bunch fresh thyme
4 tsps. browning sauce
3 tsps. red pepper flakes
2 tsps. seasoning blend
2 tsps. salt
2 tsps. hot sauce
1 clove garlic
2 bay leaves
Water to cover
6 cups beef broth
2 (15 oz.) cans lima beans, drained

Directions:

1. Combine oxtails, onions, green onions, thyme, browning sauce, red pepper flakes, seasoning blend, salt, hot sauce, garlic, and bay leaves in a large pot.
2. Let marinate in the refrigerator, stirring as often as you can, 8 hours to overnight.
3. Place pot over medium heat.
4. Pour in enough water to cover the oxtails. Simmer for 2 hours.
5. Add beef broth and cook until oxtails are tender, about 2 hours 45 minutes.
6. Add lima beans and cook until heated through, about 15 minutes. Discard thyme and bay leaves.

Diri ak Djon Djon (Haitian Black Mushroom Rice)

Ingredients:

1 cup canola oil
1 Scotch bonnet chile pepper, chopped
2 cubes black mushroom-flavored bouillon
1 cube chicken bouillon
1 cube seasoning bouillon
2 tbsps. crushed red pepper
2 tbsps. onion powder
2 tbsps. kosher salt
2 tbsps. ground black pepper
1 tbsp. ground thyme
3 tbsps. minced garlic
2 cups frozen lima beans
2 (14 oz.) cans coconut milk
6 cups water
3 cups uncooked jasmine rice

Directions:

1. Heat oil in a large pot over medium heat.
2. Add Scotch bonnet pepper, bouillon cubes, red pepper, onion powder, kosher salt, black pepper, and thyme; cook and stir until cubes dissolve.
3. Add garlic and sauté for another 4 minutes. Turn up heat to medium-high; stir in lima beans and cook for 4 minutes.
4. Pour in coconut milk and bring to a boil; stir until mixture turns black.
5. Meanwhile, bring water to a boil in another pot.
6. Stir in rice and let boil for about 10 minutes. Turn heat down to medium and mix in coconut milk mixture; cook for about 7 minutes more.
7. Reduce heat to low.
8. Place a clean dishcloth over the pot.
9. Put a lid over the top and allow to steam for at least 15 to 20 minutes. Uncover and serve.

Corn and Lima Bean Salad

Ingredients:

3 cups fresh corn kernels (6 ears)
1 tbsp. olive oil
1 cup fresh baby lima beans*
1/4 cup diced roasted red bell pepper
1 tbsp. fresh basil leaves, cut into thin strips
1 tbsp. lemon juice
3/4 tsp. salt
1/4 tsp. dried crushed red pepper

Directions:

1. Sauté corn kernels in hot oil in a large skillet over medium-high heat 3 minutes or until tender; add lima beans, and cook 2 minutes.
2. Remove from heat, and let cool 10 minutes.
3. Toss together lima bean mixture, bell pepper, and next 4 ingredients in a large bowl.
4. Cover and chill 1 hour.

Chorizo and Lima Bean Scramble

Ingredients:

12 oz. fresh Mexican chorizo, casings removed
About 1 tbsp. extra-virgin olive oil
1 medium onion, halved and thinly sliced
1 red bell pepper, cut into 2-in. strips
1 can (15 oz.) lima or butter beans, drained and rinsed
3 large eggs
Salt and pepper
1 bunch cilantro with leaves and tender stems, chopped (about 2 cups)
1/2 cup crumbled queso fresco or other mild white cheese
8 corn tortillas, warmed*
Bottled hot sauce

Directions:

1. Cook chorizo in a large frying pan over high heat, breaking up chunks with a spoon and stirring occasionally, until cooked through, about 6 minutes (to keep it from sticking, you may need to add a little water and turn down the heat).
2. With a slotted spoon, lift chorizo from any oil and put in a bowl; set aside.
3. Add enough oil to pan to make about 2 tbsp. fat.
4. Add onion and pepper and cook over medium heat, stirring occa-sionally, until onion is beginning to brown, about 10 minutes.
5. Return chorizo to pan and stir in beans.
6. With a wooden spoon, make a well in the center.
7. Crack eggs into well, sprinkle with salt and pepper, and let cook un-disturbed 15 seconds; then use a spatula to softly scramble.
8. Fold eggs into the chorizo-bean mixture.
9. Top with cilantro and cheese and serve with tortillas and hot sauce.

Bahgali Polo

Ingredients:

2 1/2 pounds basmati white rice
1 (10 oz.) package frozen lima beans
1 tsp. salt
2 pounds lamb, cut into 1-inch pieces
1 tsp. ground cinnamon
Salt and ground black pepper to taste
1/2 cup butter, divided
2 onion, halved and thinly sliced
5 tbsps. dried dill weed, or more to taste
1 tbsp. hot water
1 pint plain yogurt

Directions:

1. Thoroughly rinse rice and transfer to a large bowl.
2. Pour enough water over the rice to cover by a few inches and soak for 1 hour; drain.
3. Bring a saucepan of water to a boil.
4. Cook lima beans in boiling water until tender, 7 to 10 minutes; drain.
5. Bring a pot of water to a boil.
6. Add salt and rice to the boiling water and cook until rice is partially softened, about 11 minutes; drain.
7. Season lamb with cinnamon, salt, and pepper.
8. Melt 2 tbsps. butter in a large skillet over medium-high heat.
9. Cook and stir lamb in melted butter until completely browned, about 5 minutes.
10. Use a slotted spoon to transfer lamb to a bowl.
11. Cook and stir onion in skillet until translucent, about 7 minutes. Return lamb to skillet; add dill and cooked lima beans.
12. Remove skillet from heat.

13. Melt 3 tbsps. butter in a large saucepan over medium-high heat; add 1 tbsp. hot water. Spoon about 1/3 the partially cooked rice into the saucepan.
14. Layer about half the lamb mixture over the rice layer.
15. Repeat layering 1/2 the remaining rice, the remaining lamb mixture, and finishing with the remaining rice.
16. Cut the remaining 3 tbsps. butter into cubes and arrange atop the top rice layer.
17. Place a cover on the saucepan, reduce heat to medium-low, and cook until the rice is completely tender, about 30 minutes.
18. Remove saucepan from heat and let the mixture cool for 10 minutes before serving with yogurt.

Leek and Lima Bean Soup with Bacon

Ingredients:

3 bacon slices
2 cups chopped leek (about 2 leeks)
4 cups fresh baby lima beans
4 cups chicken broth
1 cup water
2 tbsps. fresh lemon juice
1/2 tsp. salt
1/4 tsp. freshly ground black pepper
1/2 cup thinly sliced green onions
1/2 cup reduced-fat sour cream

Directions:

1. Cook bacon in a large saucepan over medium heat until crisp.
2. Remove bacon from pan, reserving 1 tbsp. drippings in pan. Crumble bacon; set aside.
3. Add leek to drippings in pan; cook 7 minutes or until tender, stirring frequently.
4. Stir in beans, broth, and water; bring to a boil.
5. Reduce heat, and simmer 10 minutes or until beans are tender.
6. Place half of the bean mixture in a blender.
7. Remove center piece of blender lid (to allow steam to escape); secure lid on blender.
8. Place a clean dishtowel over opening in blender lid (to prevent spills), and process until smooth.
9. Pour pureed bean mixture into a large bowl.
10. Repeat procedure with remaining bean mixture.
11. Stir in lemon juice, salt, and pepper. Ladle about 1 cup soup into each of 8 bowls; top each serving with 1 tbsp. onions, 1 tbsp. sour cream, and about 1 tsp. bacon.

Lima Bean Cassoulet

Ingredients:

3 garlic cloves, thinly sliced
1 tbsp. olive oil
1 small onion, coarsely chopped
3/4 cup diced carrots
1 (8-oz.) package cooked cubed ham
1 (16-oz.) can large butter beans, drained
1/2 (16-oz.) package frozen butter peas
2 1/2 cups low-sodium fat-free chicken broth
2 tsps. chopped fresh rosemary
Cornbread Crust Batter

Directions:

1. Preheat oven to 400 degrees F. Sauté garlic in hot oil in a 10-inch ovenproof skillet over medium heat 1 minute.
2. Add onion and carrots; sauté 3 to 4 minutes or until tender.
3. Add ham; cook 3 minutes.
4. Stir in beans, peas, and next 2 ingredients; bring to a boil, and cook 5 minutes.
5. Remove from heat; pour batter over ham mixture.
6. Bake at 400 degrees F for 28 to 30 minutes or until golden brown and bubbly.

Country Lima Beans

Ingredients:

2 cups dried lima beans (about 1 pound)
1 tsp. salt
1/2 tsp. freshly ground black pepper
3 bacon slices, chopped
1 cup chopped onion
1 cup finely chopped carrot
2 cups water
2 tbsps. butter, softened

Directions:

1. Sort and wash beans; place in a large Dutch oven.
2. Cover with water to 2 inches above beans; cover and let stand 8 hours or overnight.
3. Drain the beans. Return beans to pan; stir in salt and pepper.
4. Preheat oven to 300 degrees F.
5. Cook bacon slices in a large nonstick skillet over medium heat until crisp.
6. Remove bacon from pan with a slotted spoon; set bacon aside.
7. Add onion and carrot to drippings in pan; sauté 5 minutes or until golden.
8. Add onion mixture, bacon, 2 cups water, and butter to bean mixture in Dutch oven; stir well.
9. Cover and bake at 300 degrees F for 2 1/2 hours or until beans are tender, stirring every hour.

Garlic Lima Beans

Ingredients:

4 cups fresh lima beans
2 1/2 cups water
1 tbsp. olive oil
2 garlic cloves, crushed
3 thyme sprigs
1 bay leaf
1/2 tsp. sea salt
1/4 tsp. freshly ground black pepper

Directions:

1. Sort and wash beans; drain.
2. Combine beans and next 5 ingredients (through bay leaf) in a medium saucepan.
3. Bring to a boil.
4. Cover, reduce heat, and simmer 20 minutes or until tender. Discard thyme sprigs and bay leaf.
5. Stir in salt and pepper.

Greens with Lima Beans and Smoked Turkey

Ingredients:

1 1/2 cups dried baby lima beans
1 tbsp. olive oil
2 cups vertically sliced red onion
3 cups chicken broth
1 cup diced smoked turkey breast (about 6 oz.)
1/2 tsp. dried thyme
1/4 tsp. crushed red pepper
3 garlic cloves, minced
1 bay leaf
8 cups sliced collard greens (about 1/2 pound)
2 tbsps. red wine vinegar
1 (14.5-oz.) can diced tomatoes, undrained
1/4 tsp. salt
1/4 tsp. black pepper

Directions:

1. Sort and wash beans; place in a Dutch oven.
2. Cover with water to 2 inches above beans; bring to a boil, and cook 20 minutes.
3. Remove from heat; drain beans.
4. Preheat oven to 375 degrees F.
5. Heat oil in pan over medium-low heat.
6. Add onion; sauté 10 minutes.
7. Add beans, broth, and the next 5 ingredients (beans through bay leaf); bring to a boil.
8. Cover and bake at 375° for 1 hour and 15 minutes.
9. Stir in collards, vinegar, and tomatoes.
10. Cover and bake an additional 1 hour or until beans are tender, stirring occasionally.
11. Stir in salt and pepper. Discard bay leaf.
12. Garnish with thyme sprigs, if desired.

Black Bean-Quinoa Salad with Basil-Lemon Dressing

Ingredients:

1 1/2 cups uncooked quinoa
3 cups organic vegetable broth
1 (14-oz.) package reduced-fat firm tofu, cut into 1/4-inch cubes
3 tbsps. olive oil, divided
1 1/4 tsps. salt, divided
1 cup chopped fresh basil
3 tbsps. fresh lemon juice
2 tbsps. Dijon mustard
1 tsp. sugar
2 tsps. grated lemon rind
1/2 tsp. freshly ground black pepper
3 garlic cloves, minced
1 (10-oz.) package frozen baby lima beans
4 cups chopped tomato (about 3 medium)
1/2 cup sliced green onions
1/2 cup chopped carrot
1 (15-oz.) can black beans, rinsed and drained

Directions:

1. Combine quinoa and vegetable broth in a saucepan; bring to a boil over medium-high heat.
2. Cover, reduce heat, and simmer 15 minutes or until broth is absorbed and quinoa is tender.
3. Remove from heat.
4. Place tofu on several layers of paper towels; cover with additional paper towels.
5. Let stand 5 minutes.
6. Heat 1 tbsp. oil in a large nonstick skillet over medium-high heat.
7. Add tofu; sprinkle with 1/4 tsp. salt. Sauté tofu 9 minutes or until lightly browned.
8. Remove from heat; cool completely.

9. Combine remaining 2 tbsps. oil, remaining 1 tsp. salt, basil, and next 6 ingredients (through garlic) in a large bowl; stir with a whisk until blended.
10. Stir in quinoa.
11. Cook lima beans according to package directions, omitting salt and fat.
12. Cool completely.
13. Add the lima beans, tofu, chopped tomato, green onions, chopped carrot, and black beans to quinoa mixture; stir gently to combine.
14. Store, covered, in refrigerator until ready to serve.

Cranberry Lima Beans

Ingredients:

4 cups water
2 tsps. sea salt
3 pounds fresh shelled cranberry beans (about 7 3/4 cups)
1/4 cup fresh lemon juice
2 tbsps. chopped fresh cilantro
2 tbsps. extra-virgin olive oil
1/2 tsp. freshly ground black pepper

Directions:

1. Bring water and salt to a boil in a stockpot.
2. Add beans.
3. Reduce heat, and simmer 15 minutes or until beans are tender.
4. Drain.
5. Combine lemon juice and remaining ingredients in a small bowl; stir well with a whisk.
6. Combine juice mixture and beans, tossing to coat.
7. Serve at room temperature or chilled.

Succotash Cheddar Casserole

Ingredients:

2 cups frozen baby lima beans
3 bacon slices
⅔ cup finely chopped onion
1/2 cup finely chopped red bell pepper
1/2 tsp. salt, divided
2 garlic cloves, minced
2 cups fresh corn kernels (about 3 ears)
2 1/2 tbsps. all-purpose flour
1 ⅓ cups 1% low-fat milk, divided
1/4 tsp. freshly ground black pepper
3/4 cup (3 oz.) shredded reduced-fat extra-sharp cheddar cheese
Cooking spray
15 reduced-fat round buttery crackers (such as Ritz), coarsely crushed

Directions:

1. Preheat oven to 375 degrees F.
2. Cook lima beans in boiling water 5 minutes or until crisp-tender; drain.
3. Cook bacon in a large nonstick skillet over medium heat until crisp.
4. Remove bacon from pan, reserving 2 tsps. drippings in pan. Crumble bacon, and set aside.
5. Add onion, bell pepper, 1/4 tsp. salt, and garlic to drippings in pan; cook 4 minutes or until tender, stirring frequently.
6. Stir in lima beans and corn.
7. Place flour in a small bowl; gradually add 1/3 cup milk, stirring with a whisk to form a slurry.
8. Add slurry, remaining 1/4 tsp. salt, remaining 1 cup milk, and black pepper to corn mixture; cook over medium heat 2 1/2 minutes or until thick and bubbly.
9. Remove from heat.
10. Add cheese; stir until cheese melts. Spoon into an 8-inch square baking dish coated with cooking spray.

11. Sprinkle with the cracker crumbs and bacon.
12. Bake at 375 degrees F for 20 minutes or until lightly browned on top and bubbly around edges.

Lima Bean Skillet

Ingredients:

1 pound ground beef
1/2 cup chopped onion
1/2 cup chopped green sweet or red peppers
1 tsp. minced garlic
1 cup chicken broth or beef broth or water
1 14.5 oz. can diced tomatoes (could use 2 cups fresh chopped tomatoes)
1/2 cup frozen or fresh chopped okra
1 10 oz. package frozen lima beans
1/2 tsp. black pepper
1/2 tsp. salt or to taste
1/2 cup fresh or frozen corn
1 tsp. Worcestershire sauce
1/2 tsp. cumin

Directions:

1. Brown ground beef, onion, peppers and minced garlic in a skillet on top of the stove.
2. Drain.
3. Add broth, diced tomatoes, okra, Lima beans, pepper, salt, corn, Worcestershire sauce and cumin.
4. Bring to a low boil, cover and simmer on low for 35 minutes.

Baked Gigantes in Tomato Sauce

Ingredients:

1 pound dried gigantes beans or large dried lima beans (about 2 1/2 cups)
1/4 cup extra virgin olive oil
3 cups chopped onion
1 cup chopped celery
1 cup finely chopped carrot
3 garlic cloves, minced
2 tsps. dried oregano
1 (28-oz.) can crushed tomatoes, undrained
1/4 cup chopped fresh flat-leaf parsley
2 tbsps. chopped fresh or 2 tsps. dried dill
2 tsps. honey
1 1/4 tsps. salt
1/2 tsp. freshly ground black pepper
Cooking spray

Directions:

1. Sort and wash beans; place in a large Dutch oven.
2. Cover with water to 2 inches above beans; cover and let stand 8 hours or overnight.
3. Drain beans.
4. Cover with water to 2 inches above beans, and bring to a boil.
5. Cover, reduce heat, and simmer 1 hour or until beans are tender.
6. Drain beans.
7. Preheat oven to 325 degrees F.
8. While beans cook, heat oil in a large nonstick skillet over medium heat.
9. Add onion, celery, carrot, and garlic; cook 10 minutes, stirring occasionally.
10. Stir in oregano and tomatoes; simmer 10 minutes.
11. Stir in parsley, dill, honey, salt, and pepper.

12. Combine the cooked beans and tomato mixture in a 3-quart casserole coated with cooking spray.
13. Bake at 325 degrees F for 1 hour.

Lima Bean and Potato Enchiladas

Filling Ingredients:

2 tbsps. canola oil - or vegetable oil
1 large onion - finely chopped
1 large Russet potato - peeled and cubed
1 bag (12-oz.) frozen baby lima beans
1 jalapeno pepper - chopped
4 cloves garlic - chopped
1 1/2 cups vegetable broth - or chicken broth
1/4 cup chopped cilantro
Salt and freshly ground black pepper
1 cup shredded Monterey Jack cheese

Sauce Ingredients:

1 tbsp. canola oil - or vegetable oil
4 cloves garlic - chopped
2 tsps. ground cumin
2 tsps. Mexican oregano
3 tbsps. all-purpose flour
3 cups vegetable broth - or chicken broth
2 cups roasted peeled and seeded New Mexico or Hatch green chiles
1/4 cup chopped fresh cilantro
Salt and freshly ground black pepper - to taste

To Finish Ingredients:

Cooking spray
10-12 corn tortillas
8 oz. Monterey Jack cheese - shredded
Chopped cilantro
Jalapeno slices
Sliced scallion

Filling Directions:

1. Heat oil in a large saucepan over medium-high heat.
2. Add the onion and cook 5-8 minutes until onion is beginning to soften.

3. Transfer HALF the onion to another saucepan and set that one aside.
4. In the first saucepan, add the potato, lima beans, jalapeno, garlic, and vegetable or chicken broth.
5. Bring to a boil and simmer uncovered for 12-15 minutes or until the potato is tender.
6. Take it off the heat and let it stand for 5-10 minutes.
7. Using a potato masher or immersion blender, coarsely puree the filling leaving bits of potato and lima bean for texture.
8. Set aside.

Sauce Directions:

1. To the saucepan you set aside with half the onion: Add the oil, garlic, cumin, oregano and flour and cook over low heat for a minute or two. Slowly add the chicken broth, stirring constantly.
2. Add the chiles and simmer for 10 minutes on medium-low heat until the sauce is thickened. Adjust seasoning with salt and black pepper.
3. Using an immersion blender, process the sauce until smooth.

To Finish Directions:

1. Preheat oven to 375 degrees.
2. Spray a large baking dish with cooking spray.
3. Spread approximately 1 cup of sauce over the bottom of baking dish. Working in batches, place 3-4 tortillas on a plate.
4. Top with a damp paper towel.
5. Place in the microwave and heat on high for 30-45 seconds.
6. Fill each tortilla with even amounts of the filling and roll up.
7. Place on the sauce and keep rolling until all the filling is used.
8. Top with remaining sauce and cheese.
9. Cover with foil and bake 45 minutes. Uncover and continue baking another 15-20 minutes or until bubbling.

10. Garnish with chopped cilantro, jalapeno slices and scallion.
11. Serve immediately.

Pasta with Greens and Beans

Ingredients:

8 oz. orzo
2 cups lima beans.
1 big bunch spinach
1 tsp. ground black pepper
2 tsp. red pepper flakes
6 cloves garlic minced
2 heaping tbsp capers
1/2 cup parsley chopped
1/2 cup walnuts toasted in the microwave for two minutes, then chopped into smaller pieces
1 tsp. extra virgin olive oil
Juice and zest of one lemon
Salt to taste

Directions:

1. Cook the pasta per package directions until al dente.
2. While the pasta is cooking, in a saucepan, add the olive oil and garlic and heat them together, allowing the garlic flavor to infuse the oil.
3. As the garlic starts to turn color and becomes lightly blonde, add the red pepper flakes and ground black pepper.
4. Stir for a few seconds, then add the chopped Yu Choy greens and salt to taste.
5. Stir thoroughly. Don't be alarmed if the greens look like a lot-- they will wilt down quite a bit.
6. Cover the saucepan and let the greens cook about five minutes until they have wilted and cooked down.
7. Add the lima beans and stir well to mix.
8. Add the zest, capers, lemon juice, walnuts and parsley. Now add the cooked pasta and stir everything together. Check salt and add more if needed.

Asparagus & Lima Bean Pasta Salad

Ingredients:

1/2 pound of pasta of your choice (I used GF penne)
1/2 pound of green asparagus
1 can of lima beans
1/2 cup of almond flour
1 roasted bell pepper from a jar
4 cherry tomatoes (optional)
1 tbsp. white miso
2 tbsp. tahini
1/2 yellow onion
2 cloves of garlic
1 lemon, zest+juice
fresh dill to serve
Salt, pepper

Directions:

1. Prepare pasta according to package instructions.
2. Meanwhile pasta is cooking, place almond flour, bell pepper, tomatoes, miso, tahini, diced onion, garlic, lemon juice and zest (keep a little for decorating) to a blender and blend until completely smooth.
3. Add a few tbsps. of water if the sauce is too thick.
4. In a grill pan grill asparagus for 2-4 minutes or until they have grill marks.
5. Cut into smaller pieces.
6. Add drained pasta, lima beans, pasta sauce and grilled asparagus pieces to a large bowl.
7. Toss to coat everywhere.
8. Serve immediately or after chilling, garnished with extra lemon zest, dill and black pepper if desired. Enjoy!

Lima Bean Hummus

Ingredients:

1½ cups frozen baby lima beans (8 oz.)
½ cup fresh basil
1 tbsp. + 1½ tsps. fresh lemon juice
1½ tsps. tahini
1 small clove garlic
Sea salt and freshly ground black pepper, to taste

Directions:

1. In a medium saucepan combine lima beans and 1½ cups water.
2. Bring to boiling; reduce heat. Simmer, uncovered, 20 to 25 minutes or until tender.
3. Drain.
4. In a blender or food processor combine lima beans, basil, lemon juice, tahini, and garlic.
5. Cover and blend until smooth.
6. Season with salt and pepper; pulse to combine.
7. Transfer hummus to a bowl.
8. Cover and chill until ready to serve.

Lima Bean Spread

Ingredients:

3 cups cooked Camellia Brand Large Lima Beans
1/2 cup lemon juice
1 tbsp. minced garlic
2 tbsps. minced red onion
1 tsp. dried cilantro
2 tbsps. minced fresh parsley
1/2 tsp. ground cumin
1/2 tsp. cayenne pepper
1/4 tsp. black pepper

Directions:

1. Purée cooked lima beans in a food processor.
2. Add puréed beans to a large bowl, and mix in remaining ingredients until well blended.
3. Cover and chill for at least 4 hours.
4. Serve by spreading on toasted bread slices or crackers.

Fried Lima Beans

Ingredients:

1 1/2 to 2 tsp. bacon drippings
1/4 cup minced onion
1 pkg. frozen baby lima beans
2 dashes Tabasco
1/8 tsp. Accent
1/3 cup water

Directions:

1. If possible remove lima beans from freezer and hour or two before preparation.
2. In 1 to 2-quart heavy saucepan sauté onions in bacon drippings over medium-low heat. Do not burn unions. Raise heat to medium-high and add lima beans.
3. Cook about 4-7 minutes stirring 2-3 times. Some of the limas should appear slightly burned.
4. Add Tabasco, MSG (if used) and water.
5. Bring to boil, reduce heat to medium-low, cover and cook about 10 to 15 minutes, stirring occasionally and adding more water if necessary.

Lima Bean & Broccoli Casserole

Ingredients:

1 pkg. frozen baby Limas
1 pkg. frozen chopped broccoli
 1/2 pkg. dry onion soup mix
1 cup sour cream
1 can sliced water chestnuts
2 to 3 cups of Rice Krispies
2/3 stick melted butter

Directions:

1. Barely cook and drain Limas and broccoli.
2. Mix everything together but butter and Rice Krispies and put in 1 1/2 quart casserole.
3. Stir together Rice Krispies and melted butter.
4. Top casserole with Rice Krispie mixture.
5. Bake at 350 degrees F for 30 minutes.

Lima Bean And Ham Casserole

Ingredients:

1/2 cup diced onion
1/2 cup diced celery
1 tbsp. salad oil
1 cup diced cooked ham
3 cup cooked fresh or frozen lima beans
1/2 cup lima bean liquid
1/4 cup milk
1 tbsp. all-purpose flour
1 tsp. salt
1/4 tsp. pepper
Chopped parsley (optional)

Directions:

1. Sauté onion and celery in hot salad oil for 5 minutes.
2. Combine sautéed vegetables, ham and lima beans; stir gently and spoon into a lightly greased 1 1/2-quart casserole.
3. Combine lima bean liquid, milk, flour, salt, and pepper; stir well and pour into casserole.
4. Cover and bake at 350 degrees for 45 minutes.
5. Garnish with parsley, if desired.
6. Makes 6-8 servings.

Lima Beans And Mushrooms

Ingredients:

1 pkg. frozen lima beans
1 (3 oz.) can mushrooms
1 onion, chopped
1/2 tsp. sugar
1/2 cup sour cream
Salt and pepper to taste

Directions:

1. Place frozen lima beans, onion, sugar and 1/2 cup liquid.
2. Use mushroom liquid with water added.
3. Simmer 20 minutes, until most liquid is gone.
4. Add mushrooms, salt and pepper and sour cream.
5. Garnish with parsley.

Louisiana Lima Bean Soup

Ingredients:

2 cup dried baby lima beans
8 cup cold water
Ham bone
3 sm. onions, chopped
1/2 bay leaf
1 cup carrots, chopped
1/2 cup minced green pepper
1 lg. can peeled tomatoes, chopped
3 tsp. salt
1/4 tsp. pepper

Directions:

1. Wash lima beans.
2. Place in a large kettle.
3. Add water and ham bone, onions and bay leaf.
4. Cover and simmer over low heat until the beans are tender.
5. Reserve 1 1/2 cups of whole beans.
6. Put remaining beans into blender and process until consistency of thick soup.
7. Return processed beans and whole beans to pot.
8. Add carrots, green pepper and tomato.
9. Continue cooking until tender.
10. Add salt and pepper.
11. If there is any ham on the bone, cut it off and add to soup.
12. Remove bone.

Lima Bean-Corn Pie

Ingredients:

1 (10 oz.) pkg. frozen kernel corn, thawed
1 (10 oz.) pkg. frozen lima beans, thawed
1 cup grated cheddar cheese
3 green onions, chopped
3 eggs
1 1/2 cup half and half
1 tsp. salad herbs
1/2 tsp. salt
1 ready-made 9 inch pie shell

Directions:

1. In a bowl combine the corn, lima beans, cheese and onions, mixing well.
2. In a separate bowl, beat together the eggs, half and half, salad herbs, and salt until well combined.
3. Pour mixture over lima bean mixture blending well.
4. Spread evenly into prepared pie shell.
5. Bake at 350 degrees for 30-35 minutes or until pie is firm and lightly browned.

Tuna-Lima Bean Salad

Ingredients:

1 pkg. (10 oz.) frozen lima beans, cooked, drained
2 cans (6 1/2 oz. each) water-packed tuna, drained
1 cup chopped celery
1 cup sliced green onions
1/2 cup sliced black olives
1 cup Italian salad dressing
3 cloves garlic, minced or pressed
Chopped fresh parsley
Crisp lettuce (opt.)

Directions:

1. Combine lima beans, tuna, celery, onions and olives.
2. Mix Italian dressing with garlic.
3. Fold dressing into tuna mixture.
4. Turn into serving bowl.
5. Sprinkle with parsley.
6. Cover and chill for 2 to 3 hours or overnight.
7. If desired, serve over crisp lettuce leaves.

About the Author

Laura Sommers is **The Recipe Lady!**

She lives on a small farm in Baltimore County, Maryland and has a passion for food. She has taken cooking classes in Memphis, New Orleans and Washington DC. She has been a taste tester for a large spice company in Baltimore and written food reviews for several local papers. She loves writing cookbooks with the most delicious recipes to share her knowledge and love of cooking with the world.

Follow her on Pinterest:

http://pinterest.com/therecipelady1

Visit the Recipe Lady's blog for even more great recipes.

http://the-recipe-lady.blogspot.com/

Visit her Amazon Author Page to see her latest books:

amazon.com/author/laurasommers

Follow the Recipe Lady on Facebook:

https://www.facebook.com/therecipegirl

Follow her on Twitter:

https://twitter.com/TheRecipeLady1

Other Books by Laura Sommers

German Christmas Cookbook

Christmas Hot Chocolate Recipes

Christmas Fruitcake Recipes

Christmas Cookies

Christmas Pie Cookbook

Christmas Eggnog Cookbook

Christmas Coffee Cookbook

Christmas Candy Cane Cookbook

Christmas Gingerbread Recipes

Christmas Stuffing Recipes

Made in the USA
Middletown, DE
26 November 2022